NOW I CAN
PAPER
CRAFT

20 hand-crafted projects to make

Tansy Wilson

To Steve and John Bexx: thank you for all your help.

First published 2016 by
Guild of Master Craftsman Publications Ltd
Castle Place, 166 High Street, Lewes,
East Sussex BN7 1XU

Text © Tansy Wilson, 2016
Copyright in the Work © GMC Publications Ltd, 2016

ISBN 978-1-78494-244-1

Publisher Jonathan Bailey
Production Manager Jim Bulley
Senior Project Editor Sara Harper
Copy Editor Nicky Gyopari
Managing Art Editor Gilda Pacitti
Designer Ginny Zeal
Photographer Andrew Perris

Picture credits Page 2: TunedIn by Westend61/Shutterstock; page 10 (centre): Norgal/Shutterstock
Colour origination by GMC Reprographics
Printed and bound in Turkey

Contents

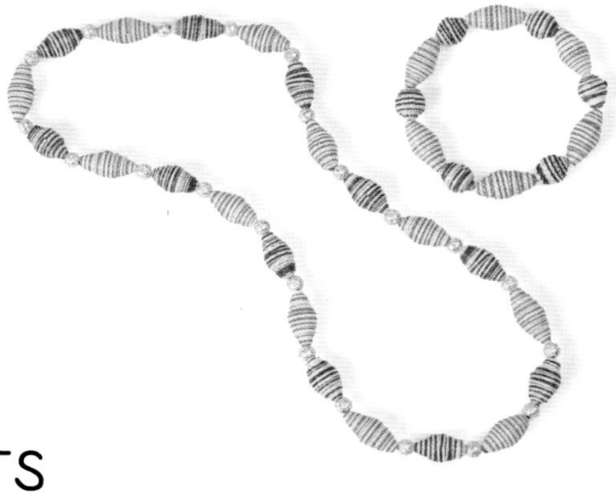

Introduction 6

THE BASICS

Tools and equipment 10

Materials 18

Techniques 26

THE PROJECTS

Pop-up monster cards 36

Paper windmill 40

Paper-plate masks 44

Dancing teddy bear 48

3D butterfly picture 52

Map mobile 56

Piggy bank 60

Pleated moths 64

Pretty wallet 68

Owl lantern 72

Rolled-paper bowl 76

Doily roses 80

Paperback hedgehog 84

Straw wreath 88

Birdie peg 92

Paper beads 96

Woven paper basket 100

Quilled flowers 104

Stag's head 108

Origami lights 112

Templates 116

Resources 124

About the author 125

Index 126

Introduction

Since I was a little girl I have loved changing paper and card into different shapes to make beautiful things. That is why I have written the projects in this book, to show you everything you need to know about the basics of paper craft. You can start off with simple monster cards and move on to more complicated projects that will take a little more time and patience. For some of them you will need a bit of help from an older brother, sister or parent. They might even want to make their own!

You'll find lots of cool things to try out, from the ancient arts of paper quilling and origami through to other classics like papier mâché or découpage. All sorts of different types of coloured or textured card and papers are used, and some of the projects include stick-on accessories, like buttons and beads, string or ribbons, to show you what other materials you can work with. There really are projects for everyone, and I hope you have as much fun making them as I did!

NOW I CAN PAPER CRAFT

NOW I CAN
PAPER
CRAFT

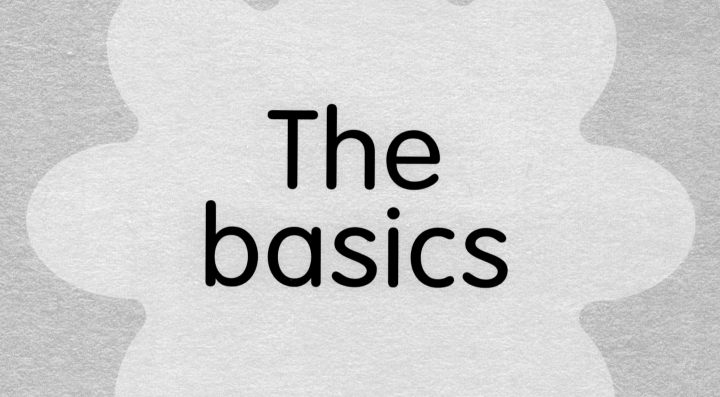

The basics

TOOLS AND EQUIPMENT

These are all the tools and equipment you will need to make the projects in this book.

Craft knife and cutting mat

An alternative to cutting straight lines other than using scissors is to use a craft knife. This has a very sharp blade and must be used with adult help. Because it is sharp, it's best to use it with a cutting mat underneath your card or paper to protect the surface you are cutting on.

Ruler

A ruler is used in quite a few of the projects to measure materials accurately. A ruler is also used for helping to cut straight lines with a craft knife. In the techniques section on page 30 you can learn how to do this.

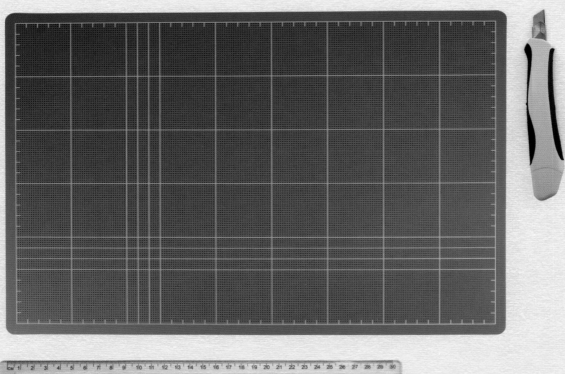

NOW I CAN PAPER CRAFT

Scissors and pinking shears

All the projects within this book require a pair of paper-cutting scissors. These have a pair of straight blades and can be whatever size you find comfortable to hold. You can also get scissors with a serrated blade called pinking shears, which cut perfect zigzag lines.

Remember, scissor blades can be quite sharp so always be careful when carrying, holding and using them.

Compass

If you put a pencil in a compass, you can push the compass point into a piece of paper or card and draw a perfect circle of many different sizes. It's a very useful tool to keep in your craft box.

Hand stamps or punches

You can buy hand-held stamps, sometimes called punches, in many different shapes and sizes. They are great for obtaining the same shape over and over again, as in the 3D Butterfly Picture project on page 52.

Hole punch

A hole punch creates a small, round hole and means you don't have to cut one out using scissors, which can be very difficult.

Pencils and pens

Every craft box should contain a selection of pens and pencils. These can be soft graphite pencils for marking and drawing templates, or coloured pencils and felt-tip pens for colouring in.

Paintbrushes

These are used in many of the projects within this book, for painting and adding water washes, and for applying white glue and varnish. You will find it helpful to have different sizes, from small to large.

Paints

It is a good idea to have a small tin of watercolour paints as well as some solid colour acrylics. These two types of paint give a very different look.

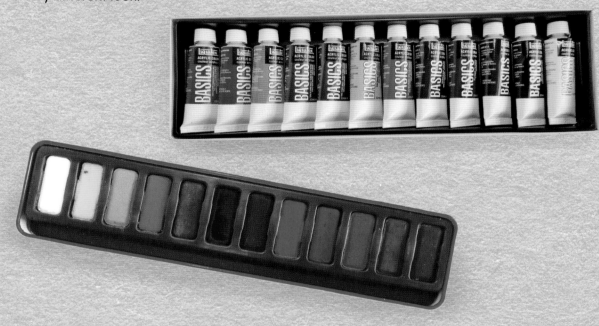

Varnish

This is important if you like the technique of découpage – see the Piggy Bank project on page 60. Varnish comes in a matt, satin or gloss finish and creates a tough coating that gives depth to the finished piece.

Glue

Glue comes in many types and four of these are used throughout this book.

Clear all-purpose adhesive

This is a completely clear glue that is great for gluing different materials together. It takes a little time to dry but is very strong.

White glue

This is a runny white glue that's good for sticking fabrics or using in techniques like papier mâché. It dries very slowly and turns clear when completely dry.

Stick glue

This is a solid glue in a stick that is easy to apply to paper and card, and which dries quite quickly.

Glue gun

This is an electric tool that heats glue to an extremely high temperature. It's great for sticking bulky items together, as in the straws in the Straw Wreath project on page 88. It dries almost immediately, but always ask an adult to use the glue gun as it can burn. The glue comes in a solid stick that you insert into the gun and it melts as the gun heats up.

Tape

Lots of different types are available. I have used double-sided tape in many of the projects instead of glue as it gives a clean, instant finish. Masking tape is useful for holding things in place temporarily. Floristry tape is a stretchy sticky tape that sticks to paper and wire and is used in the Doily Roses on page 80.

Cocktail sticks

These are great for applying glue in tricky or small areas and are also useful as a tool for starting to roll paper and card into tight coils.

Floristry wire

You will need floristry wire for the stems in the Doily Roses project on page 80. It can be bought in pre-cut lengths from craft stores.

Modelling clay

A lump of clay is really handy for keeping the cocktail sticks separate while the beads are drying in the Paper Beads project (see page 96).

Eraser

A soft white eraser is a craft-box essential for removing any pencil lines that show up on your paper and card, especially after you have drawn around templates.

Paper fasteners

These are blunt pins that have two wings that can be pulled apart to trap papers and card together. I have used them to make movable joints in the Dancing Teddy Bear project on page 48.

Pins

These come in a variety of shapes and sizes and are used in the Paper Windmill project on page 40. The longer map pins are better than regular sized pin tacks.

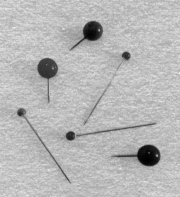

Crochet hook

This is handy for rolling papers and card around to obtain a perfect coiled spiral of paper or card, as in the Quilled Flowers on page 104.

MATERIALS

All the materials used in this book
are easy to find and cheap to buy.

Paper and card

Putting together a selection of
different types of paper and
card will help make your designs
unique. Try to have some that are
textured, others that are shiny,
and some thick as well as thin.
And, of course, include lots of
different colours, both plain
and patterned.

Tracing paper

This is a type of paper that is translucent,
which means you can see through it. You'll
need it for tracing the templates, and the
coloured kind works particularly well for
the Owl Lantern project on page 72.

Recycled paper and card

You can also reuse paper and card. Newspaper, cardboard tubes and egg boxes are used in the Piggy Bank project on page 60. Magazine pages can also be reused as colourful paper for the Pleated Moths project on page 64.

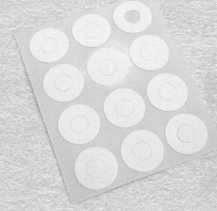

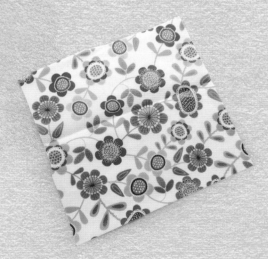

Hole reinforcers

These little sticky circles can be used to put around a hole made by a hole punch. They prevent paper and card from tearing.

Découpage paper

This is a very thin paper, almost like tissue paper, which has patterns printed on it that you can cut out. You then paste them onto shapes as a method of decoration instead of painting.

Photo frame

You can reuse and transform an old photo frame for the 3D Butterfly Picture project on page 52 or simply decorate a new one using découpage (see page 62).

Battery-operated fairy lights and tea lights

These are safe sources of light and come with either little white bulbs or ones that change colour. These lights are perfect for the Owl Lantern project on page 72.

Maps and paperbacks

Old maps or paperback books can be recycled into wonderful objects. Choose your favourite countries to cut out for the Map Mobile project on page 56. The Paperback Hedgehog on page 84 is a lovely paper sculpture made from the folded pages of an old book.

Googly eyes

These can be bought from most craft stores and are a great way to add expression and character to a project. They make the Pop-Up Monster Cards on page 36 come to life.

Curtain rings

These round rings are made in lots of different sizes and materials. I used a wooden one to hang up the Map Mobile project on page 56.

Paper plates and doilies

You can use these two materials in your projects in the same way as recycled card and paper. They are cheap and really easy to find.

Ribbons and bows

A selection of ribbons and bows finishes off a project nicely. Doesn't the Dancing Teddy Bear on page 49 look smart! Ric-rac is a type of flat, wavy ribbon used to give an attractive edge to the Pretty Wallet on page 68.

Paper straws

Often called art straws, these come in many colours. They are a great material for projects like the Straw Wreath on page 88 because they are very strong.

String

This is useful for hanging things up. Try to find some string with pretty stripes for decoration.

Pipe cleaners

These furry wires are available in lots of bright colours. Being bendy too, they are the perfect material to wrap around the pleated paper in the Pleated Moths project on page 64.

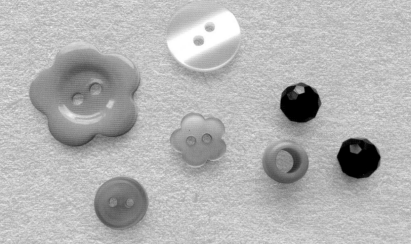

Beads and buttons

Much like ribbons and bows, it is always handy to have a selection of beads and buttons to hand.

Elastic

Elastic comes in a variety of great colours and is just the job for finishing off the Pretty Wallet project on page 68.

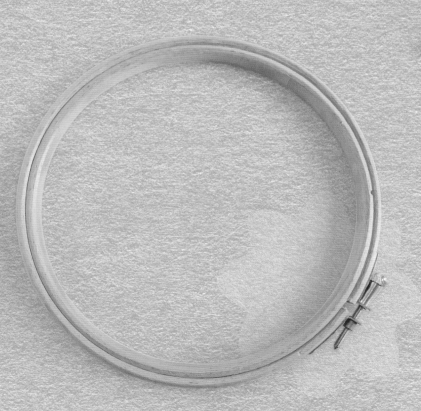

Embroidery ring

Embroidery rings are cheap to buy and really do create a professional finish to your piece. Just the inside of one is used to make the Map Mobile on page 56.

Pegs

I have used pegs for the pretty Birdie Peg project on page 92. They are just perfect when painted and make a good alternative to paper clips.

Balloons

A balloon is a great form to papier mâché over. Just take a look at how well it works for the Piggy Bank project on page 60!

TECHNIQUES

How to trace and transfer a template

This is a very simple method of tracing a template from the Templates section (see page 116) at the back of this book onto your chosen piece of paper or card.

1 If the template is a simple shape, you can place a sheet of tracing paper over the top and draw carefully around all of the lines of the template in pen or pencil.

2 Then, using scissors, cut out the shape from the tracing paper, place it onto your paper or card and draw around it using a pencil.

1

2

3 If the template is more complicated, you can transfer the image. Place a sheet of tracing paper over the template and draw carefully around all the lines of the template. Use a soft pencil such as an HB or B. If there are score lines marked, include these.

3

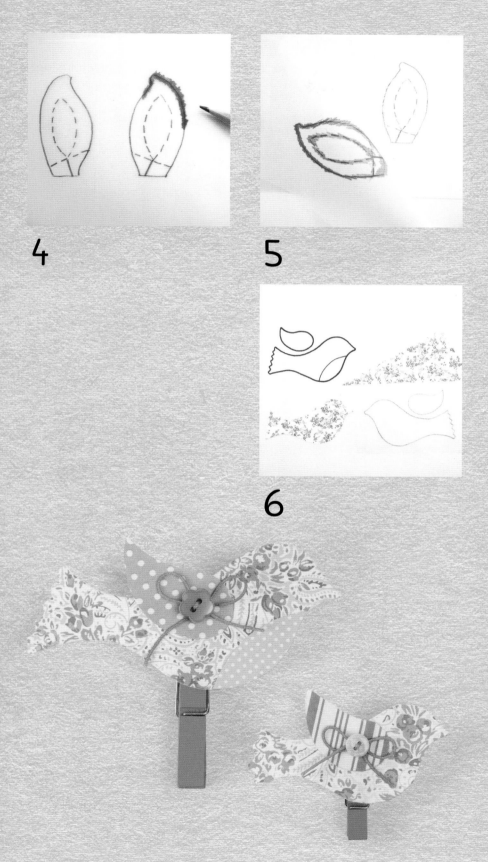

4

5

6

4 Turn the tracing paper over and place it onto a piece of paper or card. (See Step 6 if it is not symmetrical.) Hold the tracing paper with one hand to stop it moving. If it is a big template, hold it in place with some masking tape. Then, with a pencil, scribble on the reverse side of the tracing paper over where the drawn line is.

5 This process transfers the pencil line that was drawn on the tracing paper in Step 3 onto the paper or card. If your template is symmetrical, it doesn't matter if you transfer the image onto the front or back of the paper or card.

6 If your template is not symmetrical, when you trace over the template using a pencil and turn the tracing paper over ready to transfer the image, it will be facing the wrong way. So at Step 4, make sure you place the tracing paper onto the BACK of the card or paper you want to use. When you cut it out and turn the paper or card the right way round, hey presto – your shape is facing the right way again!

How to make accordion pleats

Lots of little pleats can be easily made in paper without the need for scoring lines first. These tiny folds are sometimes called concertina pleats.

1 Fold your piece of paper in half. It is much neater to make pleats from the centre out than starting from one end and going all the way to the other.

2 Decide on how wide you want your pleats to be: the narrower the width, the better the end result. Take the top half of the paper and fold it back on itself to the width you require away from the centre fold.

3 Take this same side of paper and now fold it the other way so you create another fold exactly the same width as the one in Step 2. Make sure the edges of your paper always stay in line.

4 Repeat Steps 2 and 3 to continue folding the top half of the paper back and forth until you reach the end.

5 Now you can turn the paper around. Repeat Steps 2–4, again starting at the centre fold, to make accordion pleats all the way to the other end of the sheet of paper.

1

2

3

4

5

How to score for folding

A scored line is a groove that you make in different thicknesses of card to make it easier to fold. You can use a ruler to obtain a straight line or simply score freehand into a shape, as in the Owl Lantern project on page 72. Many tools are available to make a scored line, but I have shown you the quickest and easiest method with a tool that you will already have in your craft box – a pair of scissors!

1 A pair of scissors has two blades that are very straight and sharp. However, if you look closely at your scissors, the blunt top edge of each blade is always a softer curve. This curve just before it meets the point of the blade is the perfect edge to use to score a line in a piece of card.

2 When you look at the project templates in this book, you will notice they are drawn with either a solid black line or a broken dashed line. The solid black line indicates a line you need to cut out. The broken line is one that needs to be scored so that you can make a neat fold.

3 Either using scissors or a craft knife, cut out along the solid black lines. Then place a ruler on the inside of the dashed line. Hold your scissors with the blades open and place the outside curved edge against the ruler. Make sure your scissors are now on the broken line. You may need to move the ruler in towards the line or away from it a little, depending on how thick your scissor blades are.

1

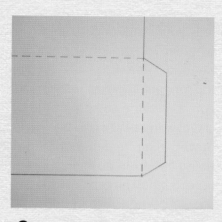

2

3

4

4 Once the scissors and ruler are in the right position, hold the ruler with one hand, keeping your fingertips away from the ruler's edge, and hold the bottom scissor blade firmly with the other hand. Keep the bottom scissor blade at an angle of no more than 45 degrees to the piece of card and move it along the ruler's edge. Once finished, you can bend along the scored line in either direction.

How to use a craft knife

A craft knife is a tool to be used with care but once you are confident with one it is an excellent way to cut perfect straight lines. Ask an adult to help you use this sharp tool.

1 A craft knife is designed with a comfortable shape to fit your hand and works whether you are left or right-handed. There is a place on the top for your finger to rest so you can control the cutting process. Usually, the blade can be moved in and out, rather than being in a fixed position. Only have a small bit of the blade showing when you cut and always slide the blade away when you have finished.

2 It is best to use a craft knife with a cutting mat underneath your paper or card. These mats come in different sizes and are made of a tough plastic that protects the surface you are cutting on. They often have measured guidelines printed on them to help you cut straight lines. Start by placing your piece of paper or card centrally on the mat.

3 Position your ruler just on the inside of the line you wish to cut first. Make sure your fingers are holding the ruler firmly in place. Spread your fingers out and along the ruler as this provides a better grip along the length of the ruler. Keep your fingertips well away from the ruler's edge.

1

2

3

4

4 Hold the craft knife in your free hand and place your index finger on the finger rest at the top of the knife. Have the blade only a little way out but make sure it clears the top of the ruler. Place the blade at the very start of the line. Applying a little pressure with your finger at

the top of the knife, press down and move the knife along the ruler's edge. It's better to use a little pressure and repeat the cut if necessary rather than press down too hard trying to cut in one go. This is particularly important if you are cutting very thick card.

NOW I CAN PAPER CRAFT

How to use paper fasteners

These little fasteners are great for joining papers and cards together without the need for glue.
It also means you can make a movable joint; see the Dancing Teddy Bear project on page 48.

1 Mark where you want the fastening to go on both pieces of paper or card. Using a hole punch, stamp out a small hole in both pieces.

2 Line up the two holes. Take one of the fasteners and feed it through both holes.

3 Turn both cards over so the head of the fastener is resting on the table and its two 'wings' are straight up in the air.

4 Using your fingers, pull the two wings apart and down.

5 Continue to pull them down until each wing rests on the surface of the paper or card.

1

2

3

4

5

How to make a pinwheel

These quick and easy decorations can be made and used just as they are for decorating cards or hanging up. They can also be used as decorations for larger pieces like the Straw Wreath project on page 88. Adding a matching colourful button finishes off your pinwheel nicely.

1 Cut out a piece of thin patterned card 8in x 3in (20cm x 7.5cm).

2 Turn the card over. With a pencil and ruler, mark out dots along the two long edges of the card at ¼in (6mm) intervals. Join the dots to create vertical lines.

3 Place a ruler along the first drawn line and, using the technique shown on page 29, score along it using the back of your scissors. Work your way across the card, scoring all of the lines.

4 Fold the card at each score line to create a pleated concertina effect. It is important that the first and last folds of card are facing upwards on the patterned side of the card.

5 Cut a piece of string and tie it tightly around the middle of the folded card, making sure the knot rests at the back of the pleats. Cut away excess string.

6 Fold the pleats in half at the knot. Cut a small strip of double-sided tape and stick it to the right side of the string. Remove the protective covering.

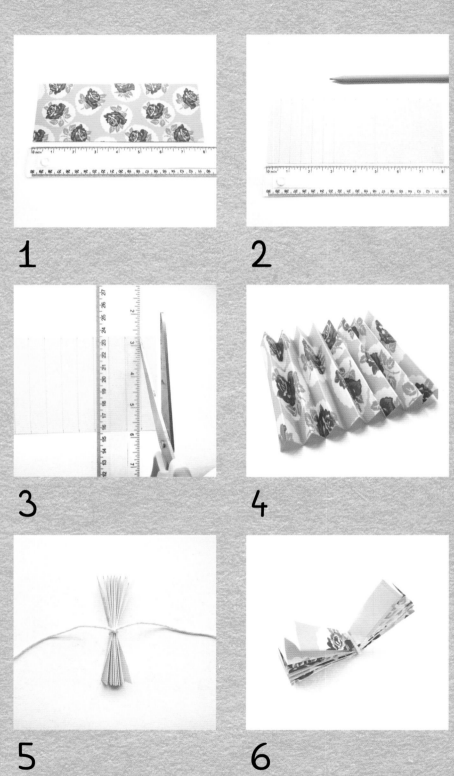

1

2

3

4

5

6

7

8

9

7 Fold the left side of the card across so you can stick it to the tape on the right side. Press them together to create half a circle of pleats.

8 Repeat Steps 6 and 7, adding another piece of double-sided tape to the right-hand edge of card from the string and bringing the left side to join it to make a circle.

9 Cut out a circle of card and glue it to the middle of the pleated circle to cover the string. Finally, add a colourful button or ribbon. Use clear all-purpose adhesive to glue it in place.

The projects

POP-UP MONSTER CARDS

Create your very own pet monster
with a pop-up mouth!

You will need:

- [ ] 1 x A4 piece of thin card
- [ ] Selection of coloured and textured cards
- [ ] Googly eyes
- [ ] Ruler
- [ ] Pencil
- [ ] Felt-tip pen
- [ ] Scissors
- [ ] Stick glue

Tip Practise drawing monsters
before you start and keep your
outlines simple.

1 Fold the A4 piece of card in half, short side to short side.

2 Using a ruler along the folded edge of the card, measure 3in (7.5cm) from the top and make a mark with a pencil. Then measure 1¼in (3cm) from this mark, away from the folded edge, and make another mark. Draw a horizontal line joining the two points.

3 Using scissors, cut along this line, starting at the folded edge.

4 Fold the card to create a small triangle shape on one side of the cut line. Now fold another small triangle from the other side.

Tip Be creative with this project and use different papers, sticky shapes and even craft feathers.

5 Unfold the triangles and open up the card. You will see the crease marks made by the triangle shapes folded in Step 4. Carefully refold these triangles, but this time fold the creases the other way to make your pop-up mouth shape.

6 Refold your card in half and press on the mouth to 'set' the shape. Keeping the card folded, use a felt-tip pen to draw one half of your monster shape on one side only, away from the folded edge. You might like to use a pencil instead of a pen so that you can rub out any mistakes. Remember that the triangle is the monster's mouth.

7 Use scissors to cut out your monster shape along the drawn line.

8 Unfold the card to reveal your symmetrical monster shape. Cut out any shapes you like in different coloured and textured card and paper to decorate it. I have cut lots of textured circles. Glue each one in place.

9 Glue on some googly eyes to make your monster come to life!

NOW I CAN PAPER CRAFT

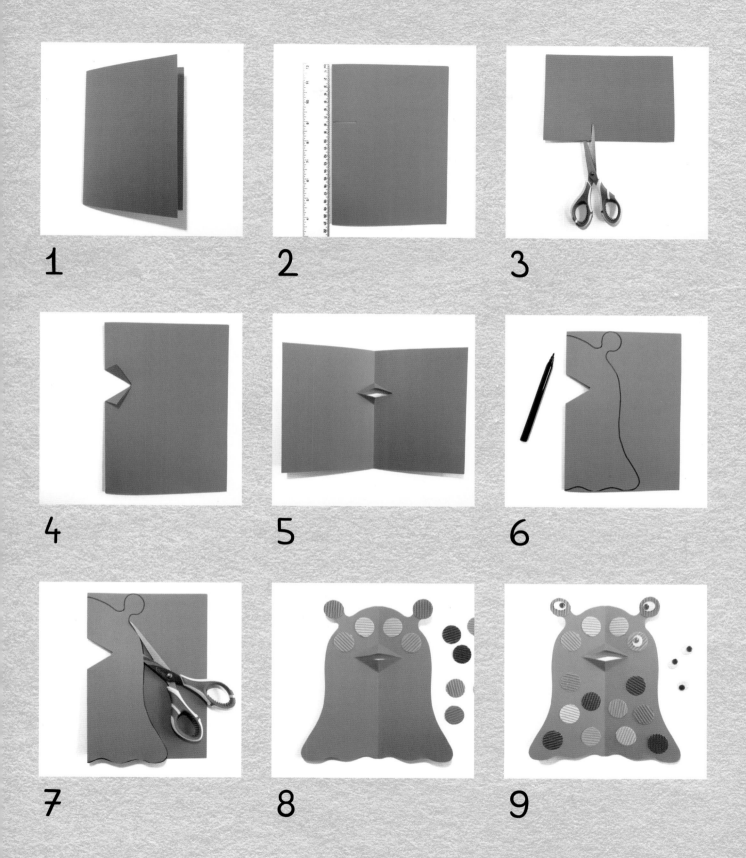

1

2

3

4

5

6

7

8

9

PAPER WINDMILL

Make a classic spinning windmill for
a summer party or table decoration.

You will need:

- [ ] 1 x 6in (15cm) square of thin patterned card or paper
- [ ] 1 x 6in (15cm) square of contrasting coloured card
- [ ] 1 x map pin
- [ ] New, unused pencil with an eraser on the end
- [ ] Ruler
- [ ] Pencil
- [ ] Scissors
- [ ] Hole punch

1 Using the ruler and pencil, draw a diagonal line from one top corner of the square of paper to the opposite bottom corner. Draw another diagonal line from the other corners to find the centre of your square.

2 Measure 1¼in (3cm) from the centre point of your square along one of the lines and mark a dot with a pencil. Repeat this step to mark a 1¼in (3cm) dot from the centre point on each line.

3 Cut along one of the diagonal lines from the corner up to the dot marked in Step 2. Repeat this step to cut along all of the diagonal lines.

4 Use the hole punch to make a hole in the right-hand corner of each triangle. Keep rotating the card after each hole so you know it's the right-hand side. Finally, punch a hole in the very centre.

5 Cut a ¾in (2cm) diameter circle out of the piece of contrasting coloured card and use the hole punch to make a hole in the centre of this circle. Take the map pin and poke it through the hole.

6 Now take your square and bend each triangle so that the holes punched at each corner also thread onto the map pin. Do one triangle at a time, and finish by threading the map pin through the hole in the centre of the square.

7 Push the tip of the map pin into the small eraser on top of the new pencil to hold your windmill in place and create a stick to hold onto.

Tip You can use a pin tack instead of a map pin – the longer the pin, the better the spin!

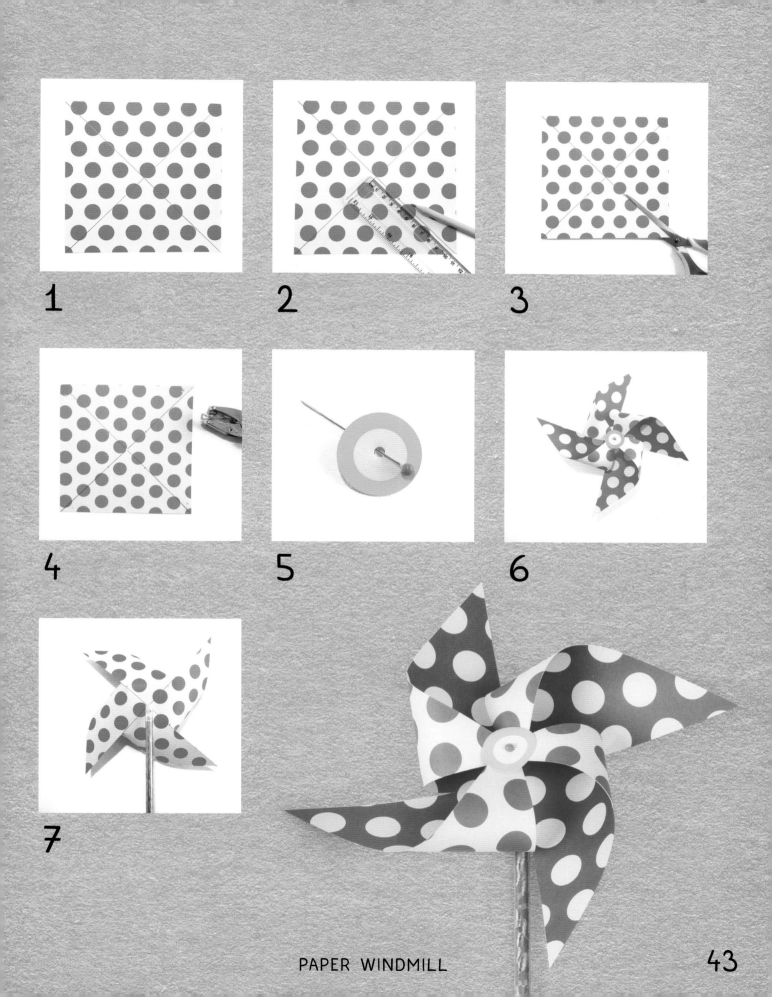

1

2

3

4

5

6

7

PAPER WINDMILL

PAPER-PLATE MASKS

Get really creative with your painting to make your favourite animal faces.

You will need:

- ☐ 1 x 7in (18cm) diameter paper plate
- ☐ Acrylic paints in the colours you want to paint your mask
- ☐ Felt-tip pen
- ☐ Hole punch
- ☐ Paintbrush
- ☐ Thin elastic
- ☐ Scissors

Tip Spare paper plates can be used to mix your paints on!

1 To make the lion shown here, place your plate with the rim facing up. Use the pen to draw onto your plate the overall face shape, two eyeholes and two ears. You might like to use a pencil instead of a pen so that you can rub out any mistakes.

2 Using your scissors, completely cut out the eyeholes and bottom edge of the face shape. Partially cut out the ears so you can bend them forwards to make them more realistic.

3 Use the hole punch to punch out a small hole either side of the mask just below eye level for your elastic.

4 Now you can go wild and paint your animal face. For the lion, paint a light brown all over the face then use dark brown all around the edge of the plate. Make sure the paint goes in between the grooves on the rim. Paint around the edges of the ears and paint a nose. Leave to dry.

5 When the dark brown paint is dry, use the light brown colour from step 4 and brush lightly across the rim of the plate. The paint will only go on the high points of the plate, leaving a perfect stripy lion's mane. You can paint on details for the eyes and cheeks.

6 Cut a piece of elastic approximately 15in (38cm) long and thread one end through one of the holes punched out in Step 3. Tie a knot. Pass the other end through the hole on the other side. Before tying another knot, make sure it fits around your head. Cut away any excess elastic.

Tip Turning the paper plate over so the rim faces down creates a different face shape. You can also cut out ears from the discarded plate rim.

NOW I CAN PAPER CRAFT

1

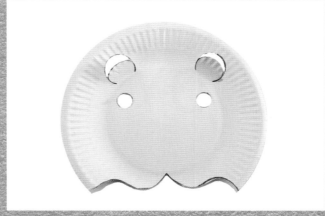

2

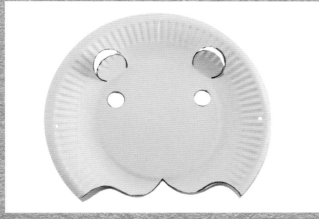

3

4

5

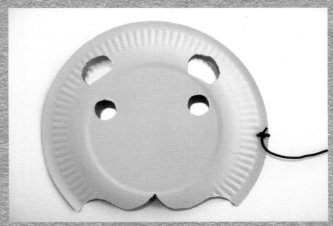

6

DANCING TEDDY BEAR

Find the template on page 120

Otherwise known as a 'Jumping Jack', this moving puppet is fun to make.

You will need:

- [ ] 1 x A4 sheet of thin card
- [ ] 1 x A4 sheet of animal-print card
- [ ] 4 x paper fasteners
- [ ] Pencil
- [ ] Tracing paper
- [ ] Scissors
- [ ] Hole punch
- [ ] Coloured pencils
- [ ] Stick glue
- [ ] Thin string
- [ ] Bead (make sure the string can fit through the hole of the bead)
- [ ] Piece of colourful ribbon to make a bow

1 Trace over all the shapes on the template on page 120, using the technique shown on page 26. Remember to also trace where the holes go. Cut out the shapes then draw round them on your sheet of thin card. Alternatively, you can photocopy the template onto thin card, then cut it out.

2 Cut out all the shapes using scissors. This will be easier to do if you roughly cut the teddy-bear shapes into smaller pieces first.

3 Use the hole punch to punch out all the small holes on the body, arms and legs.

4 Cut out a large oval from the animal-print card to make a patch for the teddy bear's tummy. Use stick glue to glue in place on the body shape.

5 Cut smaller ovals from the same animal-print card to make patches for his paws and ears. Again, use stick glue to secure them in place. Now get creative with your coloured pencils and add texture for his fur – and draw on a cute face, too!

6 Attach the arms and legs to the body by pushing paper fasteners through the bottom holes at the arm and leg joints and through the body (see How to use paper fasteners, page 31). Turn the puppet over and gently prise the two wings apart, pressing them down.

7 Cut a piece of string 12in (30cm) long. Working on the back of your teddy, thread one end through the top hole at the arm and tie a knot to secure in place. Thread the other end of the string across to the other arm, through the top hole and tie another knot. Cut away any excess string. Repeat this step to add string across the legs.

8 Cut a piece of string 15½in (40cm) long and tie one end to the middle of the piece of string going across the arms (done in Step 7). Then using this same length of string, feed it down the puppet and tie it to the middle of the piece of string going across the legs (done in Step 7). The remainder of this length of string can hang down between the teddy bear's legs. Thread a bead onto the bottom of this length of string and tie a knot to secure the bead. Add a loop of string to the hole at the top of the head to hang your puppet up. Finally, you can make a bow tie from a piece of ribbon and glue into place.

Tip Do not squash your paper fasteners too much. Fold them back gently so your puppet's arms and legs will move easily.

NOW I CAN PAPER CRAFT

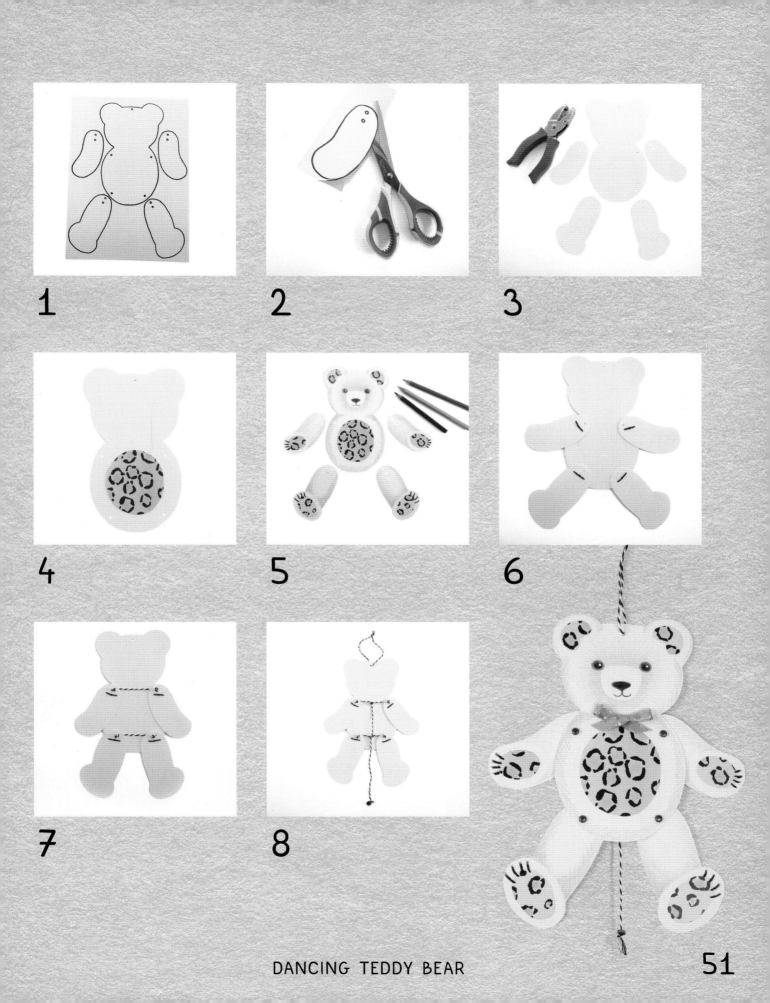

1

2

3

4

5

6

7

8

DANCING TEDDY BEAR

3D BUTTERFLY PICTURE

Use watercolour paints on paper to make beautifully coloured butterflies, then frame them to put on the wall.

You will need:

- [ ] 1 x A4 piece of thin black card
- [ ] 1 x A3 sheet of white cartridge paper
- [ ] 1 x A4 piece of textured card (e.g. ribbed, flecked, embossed)
- [ ] Watercolour paints
- [ ] Recycled photo frame
- [ ] Butterfly punch
- [ ] Pencil
- [ ] Ruler
- [ ] Craft knife
- [ ] Cutting mat
- [ ] Soft paintbrush
- [ ] Jar of water
- [ ] Scissors
- [ ] White glue

1 Measure the width of the butterfly punch and mark this measurement on one of the short sides of the cartridge paper with a small pencil dot. Also mark this measurement on the other short side. Take the ruler and the pencil and draw a line to connect the two dots. Using a craft knife against the ruler's edge on a cutting mat, cut carefully along this drawn line so you are left with a long strip of paper (see How to use a craft knife, page 30).

2 Dip a soft paintbrush in water and coat the surface of the strip of paper with a wash of water. Using whatever colours you like, dip the paintbrush into the watercolour paints, one at a time, and make a bright, colourful pattern on the paper. Leave to dry completely.

3 When the painted paper is dry, take the butterfly punch and stamp out your first colourful butterfly. Leave to one side and then use scissors to cut off the butterfly hole that's left behind.

4 Repeat Step 3 to stamp out as many colourful butterflies out of the strips of paper as you want to use, repeating Steps 1 and 2 to cut out and paint more strips if required. Use the butterfly punch to stamp out the same number of butterflies out of the thin black card.

5 Take a colourful butterfly and fold it in half. Add a drop of glue to the centre of one of the black butterflies and glue the folded butterfly on top of it. Repeat this step to glue each colourful butterfly onto a black one, and leave to dry.

6 Remove the glass from an old photo frame. Cut a piece of textured card the same size as the photo and place it where the photo would have been. You can use a dot of glue to hold the card in place if necessary.

7 Lay all your butterflies in a pattern across the inside of the frame until you are happy with the design. Starting at one end, add a drop of glue to the underside of the first butterfly and glue in position. Continue to work your way across the frame, gluing them all in place one at a time.

8 When the glue has completely dried, use your fingers to tweak all the butterfly wings, refolding them away from the black card.

Tip Add a butterfly to the outside of the frame so it looks like it might fly away!

1

2

3

4

5

6

7

8

MAP MOBILE

Find the template on page 118

Cut out lots of different countries from around the world and turn them into a mobile for your room.

You will need:

- [ ] 1 x large folded paper world map, 32in x 47in (81cm x 119cm)
- [ ] 1 x 2in (5cm) wooden curtain ring
- [ ] 1 x 6in (15cm) embroidery ring
- [ ] Tracing paper
- [ ] Card for making stencil
- [ ] Pencil
- [ ] Scissors
- [ ] Eraser
- [ ] Stick glue
- [ ] White glue
- [ ] String

1 Trace over the heart stencil on page 118 using the technique shown on page 26 and cut it out. Draw around the shape on a piece of card and cut it out. Now place the card heart over the world map and draw around it using a pencil. Move the heart over a different place and draw around it again. Keep doing this until you have 66 hearts.

2 Cut your map into smaller pieces to make it easier to handle, being careful not to cut across the hearts. Carefully cut out all of the heart shapes. Use the eraser to rub out any pencil lines that are still visible on your hearts.

3 Cut six pieces of string each approximately 40in (1m) in length. Tie five of them one by one onto the wooden curtain ring. Try to tie them so you only have a short piece of excess string hanging down approximately ½in (1cm) in length alongside the long lengths. (You can always trim the short piece using scissors.) Tie on the sixth piece of string, this time making sure you leave at least 4in (10cm) of excess string hanging down.

4 Hold the 4in (10cm) length of excess string and wrap it around the top of all of the long lengths of string. As you wrap it round, try to trap all of the short ½in (1cm) excess lengths underneath so they are not visible. Keep wrapping this 4in (10cm) piece of string until you have no more left. Add some white glue to the end and leave to dry.

Tip Once the glued hearts are dry, use your scissors to trim the edges and remove any white bits that are showing.

5 Cut another piece of string approximately 8in (20cm) long and tie it to the top of your curtain ring to make a loop at the top so that you can hang up your mobile. Take one of the six long strings hanging from the curtain ring and measure approximately 6in (15cm) down from the ring. At this point, tie it onto your embroidery ring with a loose single knot. Take another string and also loosely tie it to your embroidery ring, opposite where the first string is tied. Keep moving around the ring, attaching the remaining four long strings to it in the same way, and keep the knots loose. Adjust the knots until you get the ring to hang horizontally. When it is horizontal, tighten each knot and add another knot to secure it in place.

6 You will now be left with six lengths of string hanging from the embroidery ring, all around 24in (60cm) in length or longer. Pick up one of the cut-out hearts and cover the back of it entirely with stick glue. Place it glue side up close to the embroidery ring and lay one of the long strings straight down the centre over the top.

7 Pick up another cut-out heart and place it with the picture side up directly over the glued heart and string, matching up the shapes as best you can. Press firmly to stick the two hearts together and sandwich the string in between.

8 Repeat Steps 6 and 7 in order to glue six pairs of hearts to one string and then five pairs of hearts to the next string along. Keep alternating so that you end up with all of the strings covered in either five or six hearts.

9 Using scissors, cut any remaining length of string away from the very bottom heart. Do this for each string.

1

2

3

4

5

6

7

8

9

MAP MOBILE

PIGGY BANK

Make a pretty papier-mâché piggy bank
to keep your savings in!

You will need:

- [ ] 1 x old newspaper
- [ ] 1 x piece of découpage paper
- [ ] 1 x oval-shaped balloon
- [ ] 1 x cardboard tube (from a toilet roll, for example)
- [ ] 1 x egg box
- [ ] Masking tape
- [ ] Scissors
- [ ] White glue
- [ ] Small container (a plastic cup, for example)
- [ ] Paintbrush
- [ ] Craft knife
- [ ] White acrylic paint
- [ ] Varnish

1 Take the newspaper and cut or tear it into lots of small squares. I used scissors, but if you tear the newspaper you get a smoother finish.

2 Blow up a balloon to the size you want your piggy bank body. Ours is about 6in (15cm) long. Water down some white glue approximately 1 part water to 3 parts glue in a small container and paint all over the balloon using a paintbrush. Stick on some of the small newspaper squares, adding more glue and overlapping them as you go. Continue adding the small squares until they completely cover the balloon. Leave to dry.

3 To make the pig's legs, cut the cardboard roll in half so you have two small fat tubes. Then cut each fat tube open and cut it in half lengthways so you are left with four pieces of card. Take one piece and form a tube approximately ¾in (2cm) in diameter. Secure with masking tape and do the same with the other pieces to make four tubes.

4 Using scissors, cut slits approximately halfway down the length of each tube, splaying the card out. Try to cut the same lengths on each tube.

5 Using scissors, cut out one of the cups from an egg box for the piggy's nose, then cut another cup in half to make the ears. Use masking tape to stick the nose over the tied end of the balloon. Then stick on the ears and each leg with the splayed part upwards.

6 Using the watered-down white glue that you prepared in Step 2, paint a layer all over your first layer of papier mâché, as well as over the legs, nose and ears. Stick on more small squares of newspaper. Continue to overlap the small squares until they completely cover the surface. Leave to dry. Repeat this step several times until you have a very solid piggy shape.

7 When you have a completely dry solid shape, take the craft knife and carefully make a slit along the top of your piggy's back. The balloon should have already deflated and you will now be able to pull it out.

8 Using a clean paintbrush, paint your piggy all over with white acrylic paint and leave to dry. Using scissors, cut out lots of shapes from the découpage paper.

9 Pick up a découpage shape and place onto your piggy. Use the watered-down white glue to paint the glue all over the shape so it lies completely flat on the surface. Continue adding shapes all over your piggy until completely covered then leave to dry. Finish by applying at least two coats of varnish to your piggy bank. Leave the varnish to dry between coats.

Tip Tie a piece of string to the balloon so you can hang it up to dry between each layer of papier mâché.

NOW I CAN PAPER CRAFT

1

2

3

4

5

6

7

8

9

PLEATED MOTHS

Make some colourful moths to decorate
your bedroom lamp.

You will need:

- [ ] 1 x old magazine
- [ ] 3 x pipe cleaners
- [ ] Scissors
- [ ] Ruler
- [ ] Compass
- [ ] Pencil
- [ ] Stick glue
- [ ] Clear all-purpose adhesive

1 Using the ruler and pencil, measure and draw a square 5in x 5in (13cm x 13cm) over one of the magazine pictures. Now, using the compass and pencil, draw a circle 3¼in (8cm) in diameter over a picture in another colour or pattern. Finally, draw two small ovals approximately 1½in (4cm) high and ¾in (2cm) wide. Cut out all the shapes.

2 Using the stick glue, stick the circle to one of the corners of the square, as shown in the picture. Glue the two ovals on the top section of the square.

3 Take the top corner of the square, fold it down in half and make a firm crease.

4 Pleat the paper to make accordion pleats as small as you can on the top section of the square, working all the way to the very tip (see How to make accordion pleats, page 28). The smaller the pleats, the better your finished moth will look.

5 Once the top section of the square has been completely folded, continue pleating in the same way all the way down to the bottom of the circle. Again, keep the pleats as small as possible.

6 Cut a 1½in (4cm) length off a pipe cleaner and lay this small piece across the very top of your pleats. Cut 3¼in (8cm) off the remaining pipe cleaner and fold this piece in half. Place the folded pipe cleaner over the top pipe cleaner and across all the pleats so it hangs down at the centre.

7 Twist the two ends of the folded pipe cleaner together so they form the body, trapping all the pleats together along with the piece of pipe cleaner you laid across the top. Trim the twisted section if it is too long. Bend the top pipe cleaner up to make two antennae. Finally, open up the pleats. Make two more moths in the same way. You can glue the moths to your bedroom lamp with all-purpose adhesive or simply hang them up in your room.

Tip Old travel brochures often have many pretty coloured photographs to cut out.

NOW I CAN PAPER CRAFT

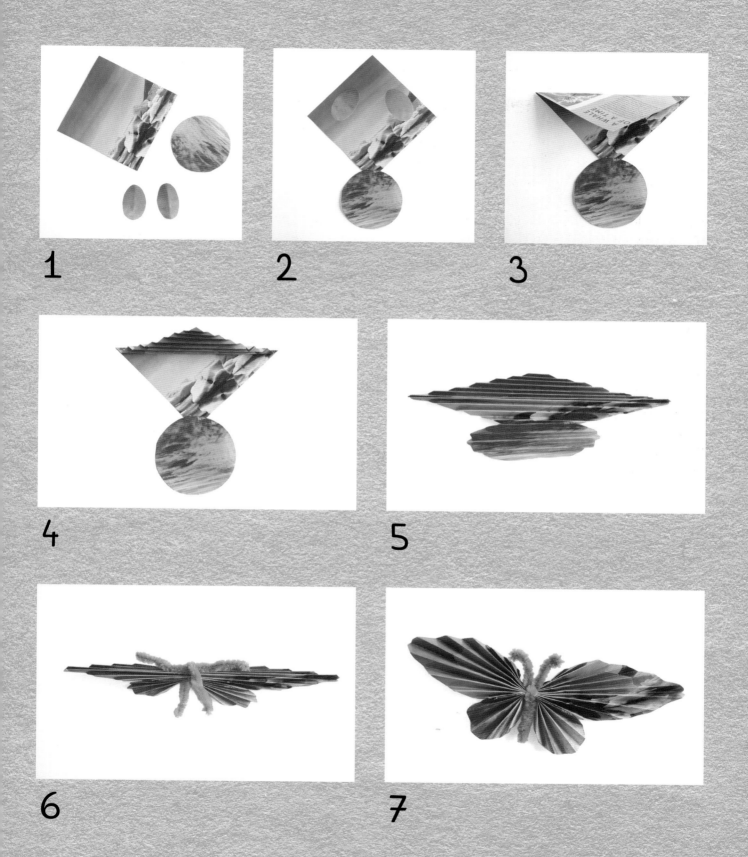

1

2

3

4

5

6

7

PRETTY WALLET

Keep your money or special messages safe in this pretty patterned wallet.

Find the template on page 117

You will need:

- ☐ 1 x A4 piece of card with pattern on both sides
- ☐ Tracing paper
- ☐ 1 x ¾in (2cm) button
- ☐ Cord elastic (make sure it fits through the holes of your button)
- ☐ Ric-rac ribbon
- ☐ Ruler
- ☐ Pencil

- ☐ Craft knife
- ☐ Cutting mat
- ☐ Scissors
- ☐ Hole punch
- ☐ 1 x hole/ring reinforcer
- ☐ White glue
- ☐ Stick glue
- ☐ Sticky tape

1 Trace over the template on page 117 using the technique shown on page 26. Transfer it onto the patterned card. Draw it onto the side that will be the inside of the wallet. Alternatively, photocopy the template onto the card, then cut it out.

2 Use a craft knife along the ruler's edge to cut out the straight edges. Make sure your card is on a cutting mat so you do not mark the table (see How to use a craft knife, page 30).

3 Use scissors to cut out the curves. Place the ruler along the fold lines and, using the blunt edge of the scissors, carefully score a line (see How to score for folding, page 29). Repeat the scoring process along the other three fold lines.

4 Fold the card into the envelope shape and then press along the fold lines so it will fold neatly together.

5 Mark a dot on the inside of the envelope where you want to place your button. Remember: the button needs to be below the envelope flap when it is closed. Use the hole punch to make a hole at this point. Add a hole reinforcer so that the card won't tear.

6 Thread a 4in (10cm) length of cord elastic through both holes in the button, from the back to the front and then back through the second hole. Then thread both ends through the hole in the envelope that you made in Step 5. Use white glue to stick the elastic in place on the card in a neat line. When it is completely dry, cut any excess away.

7 Cut a 2in (5cm) length of cord elastic and form a small loop that will easily fit over your button. Use white glue to stick this loop onto a piece of ric-rac that is 12in (30cm) in length. Leave long ends of elastic hanging over the edge and stick tape to these pieces to hold them in place while drying. Once dry, cut away the excess elastic.

8 Use white glue to stick the ric-rac onto the front curved edge of your wallet, making sure that the loop is in the centre and will go over your button. Leave to dry and then cut away any excess ric-rac using scissors.

9 Apply stick glue to the tabs either side of the body of the envelope and fold back into its final shape. Press firmly and leave to dry.

Tip Using buttons and ric-rac that match the pattern on your card will add a nice finishing touch.

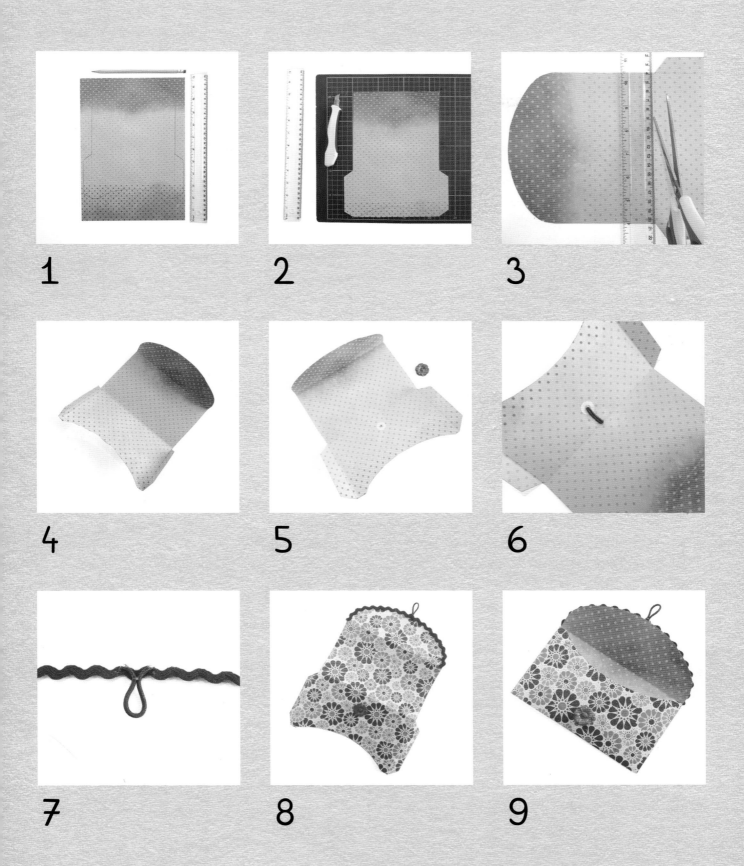

1

2

3

4

5

6

7

8

9

OWL LANTERN

This cute owl has a tracing-paper belly so that it glows in the dark.

Find the template on page 119

You will need:

- [ ] 1 x A4 sheet of thin dark-coloured card
- [ ] 1 x A4 sheet of thin light-coloured card
- [ ] 1 x A4 sheet of coloured tracing paper
- [ ] 1 x A4 sheet of yellow card
- [ ] 1 x A4 sheet of black card
- [ ] Plain tracing paper
- [ ] Ruler

- [ ] Pencil
- [ ] Craft knife
- [ ] Cutting mat
- [ ] Scissors
- [ ] 1 x ¾in (20mm) hole stamp
- [ ] Compass
- [ ] Double-sided tape
- [ ] Stick glue
- [ ] Battery-operated tea light

Tip Place the owl over a battery-operated tea light. Never use a real flame with this lantern.

1 Trace over the template on page 119 and transfer it onto the back of the sheet of dark-coloured card, using the technique shown on page 26. Alternatively, photocopy the template onto the back of the dark-coloured card. Using a craft knife along a ruler's edge, cut out all of the straight edges, including those on the belly shape in the middle (see How to use a craft knife, page 30). Now use scissors to cut out the curved edges.

2 Using the back of the scissors along the ruler's edge, score the two straight lines where marked. Then, again using the back of the scissors but this time without the ruler, carefully score along the curves (see How to score for folding, page 29).

3 Gently fold the card along the scored lines to 'set' the shape. Open the card back out and cut a piece of coloured tracing paper large enough to cover the cut-out belly hole. Use the stick glue around the edges of the coloured tracing paper to glue it in place. If the tracing paper has a pattern, make sure it is nicely placed when looking at the owl from the front.

4 Cut a strip of double-sided tape and stick it along the tab. Peel off the backing and re-fold the card, sticking the card together where the tab is. Press firmly to hold. Gently re-fold along the curved score lines to fold the top of the owl's head in place. Fold the back eye-shaped piece down first so the front curve folds over the top of it. Then you won't see the open edge from the front.

5 Using the hole stamp, stamp out 16 circles in the light-coloured card. Then stamp out three dark-coloured circles and cut these circles in half with the scissors to make semi-circles.

6 You need eight circles per wing in the light-coloured card. Starting from the bottom of the wing, use the stick glue to add one circle. Then working upwards, glue two circles, slightly overlapping each other, then three circles and finally another two.

7 Repeat Step 6 to add the remaining eight light-coloured card circles to the other side to make a matching wing. Glue the six dark-coloured semi-circles in a line next to each other along the top of the wings, just covering the top edge of the wings and tracing paper.

8 Use the hole stamp to stamp out two circles from the black card. Use the pencil and compass to draw two larger circles on the yellow card then cut them out. Cut out a beak shape from the yellow card.

9 Stick one of the black circles onto the middle of the yellow circle. You can also add a little white dot to make the eye look twinkly. Repeat this to make the other eye. Stick the eyes into the space left above the semi-circles and then add the beak in the middle.

NOW I CAN PAPER CRAFT

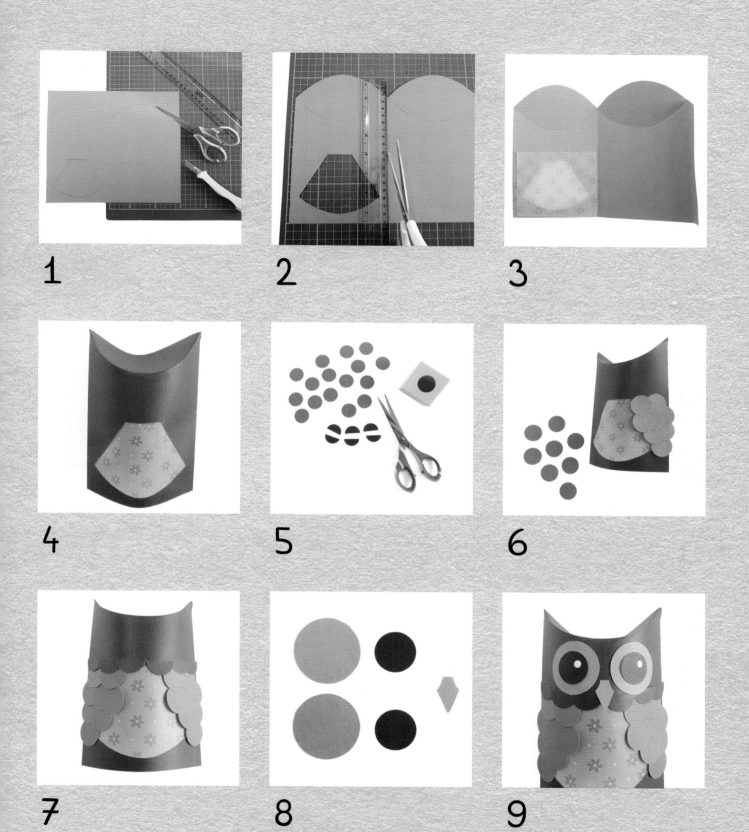

1

2

3

4

5

6

7

8

9

ROLLED-PAPER BOWL

Get rolling and make a beautiful bowl
for all your bits and pieces.

You will need:

- [ ] 1 x A4 scrapbook pad of sugar paper
- [ ] Knitting needle, crochet hook, pen or other thin cylindrical object
- [ ] Ruler
- [ ] Craft knife
- [ ] Cutting mat
- [ ] Scissors
- [ ] Double-sided tape
- [ ] White glue
- [ ] Elastic band

Tip You can use other types of paper or even old magazines – 20 A4 pages make a bowl about 8in (20cm) in diameter. Use fewer or more sheets, depending on how large you want your bowl.

1 Cut 20 pages out of the scrapbook. I have used four different colours so I have cut five pages of each colour. Measure as many 2in (5cm) wide strips out of the length of each page as possible. Place on a cutting mat and, using a craft knife along the ruler's edge, cut them out using the technique shown on page 30.

2 Using the back of your scissors, make four evenly spaced score lines along the length of each strip (see How to score for folding, page 29). This will make it a lot easier to fold your strips.

3 Fold each paper strip along the scored lines, folding the outer edges to the middle score line first, and then folding the entire strip in half lengthways along the middle line. Press firmly to make the strip as flat as possible.

4 Add a small amount of double-sided tape to the end of each folded strip. Join the folded strips to each other, making sure the open fold is always on the same side. Join at least five pieces together at a time so you are left with at least 20 very long strips of joined folded paper.

5 Take one long strip and start to tightly roll one end around a crochet hook or other cylindrical object.

6 Once the spiral has started to form, slide the rolled paper off the cylindrical object and continue rolling the paper around itself using your fingers.

7 When you have come to the end of one strip, join the next strip to it with more double-sided tape and continue to spiral the paper around until you have used all of your strips. Use an elastic band to keep the coil in place while you are sticking strips together.

8 Use more tape to secure the very last strip to the entire coil. Then using your fingers, very gently start to ease the strips up and away from the centre of the spiral.

9 When you are happy with the shape and size of the bowl, paint the entire surface with white glue to stick all the strips together. Leave to dry. You may need to add a second coat of glue to make the bowl stronger.

Tip Make smaller spirals and join them together for a different look.

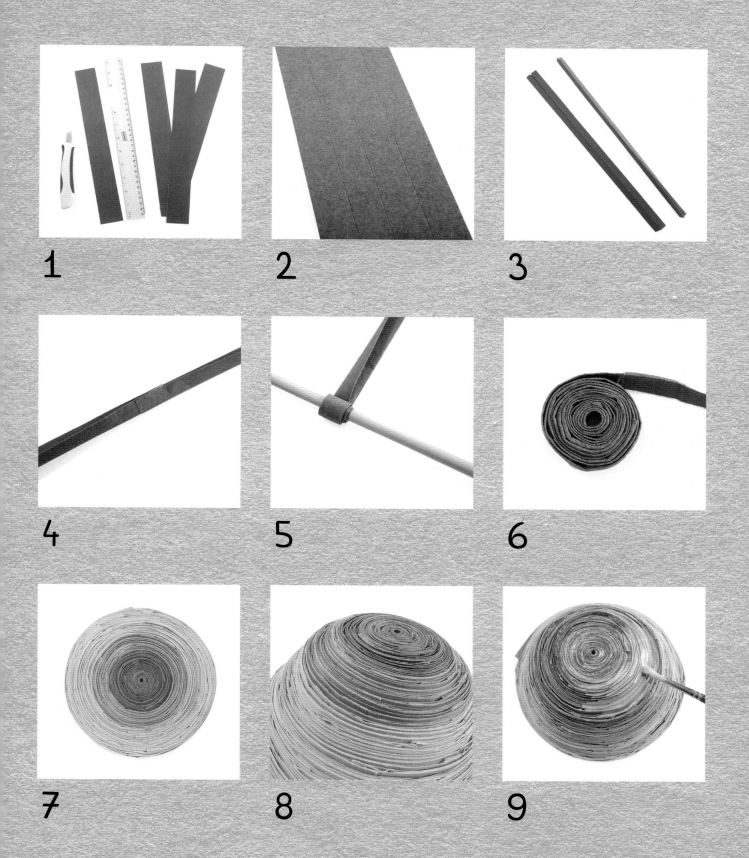

1

2

3

4

5

6

7

8

9

DOILY ROSES

Turn pretty paper doilies into a bunch of beautiful roses in this easy project.

You will need:

- [ ] Paper lace doilies (minimum 8½in/22cm in diameter)
- [ ] 10-inch (25cm) pre-cut lengths of green floristry wire, SWG 18 (AWG 16, 1.2mm), same quantity as doilies
- [ ] Floristry tape
- [ ] Scissors
- [ ] Cocktail stick (optional)

1 Using scissors, cut a straight line from the outer edge of the doily towards the centre. Cut out a circle approximately ½in (1cm) away from the inner lace edge. This solid border will give your flower a bit more strength.

2 Starting at the cut end, start to coil the doily around itself, creating a tight spiral.

3 Keep rolling the doily around itself to form a larger spiral cone shape. Once you have started the spiral, this is very easy to do.

4 Carefully feed the end of a piece of floristry wire through the centre of the cone from the bottom of the rose so you can just see the tip of the wire in the centre of the spiral. Cut off a 4in (10cm) piece of floristry tape and wrap it around the bottom of the doily cone, trapping both the cone and wire in place.

5 Wrap the tape around a few times as tightly as possible and then work the tape down and onto the length floristry wire so at least 2in (5cm) of the top of the wire is covered. You can cut a few pieces of tape to repeat this step to attach the doily very securely to the wire stem.

6 Cut a few small slits into the top edge of the doily and then bend back sections and manipulate them with your fingers to make it look like individual petals of a rose. Repeat Steps 1 to 6 to make as many doily roses as you like.

Tip To start the spiral off, wrap the cut end of the doily around a cocktail stick and use it like a rolling pin.

NOW I CAN PAPER CRAFT

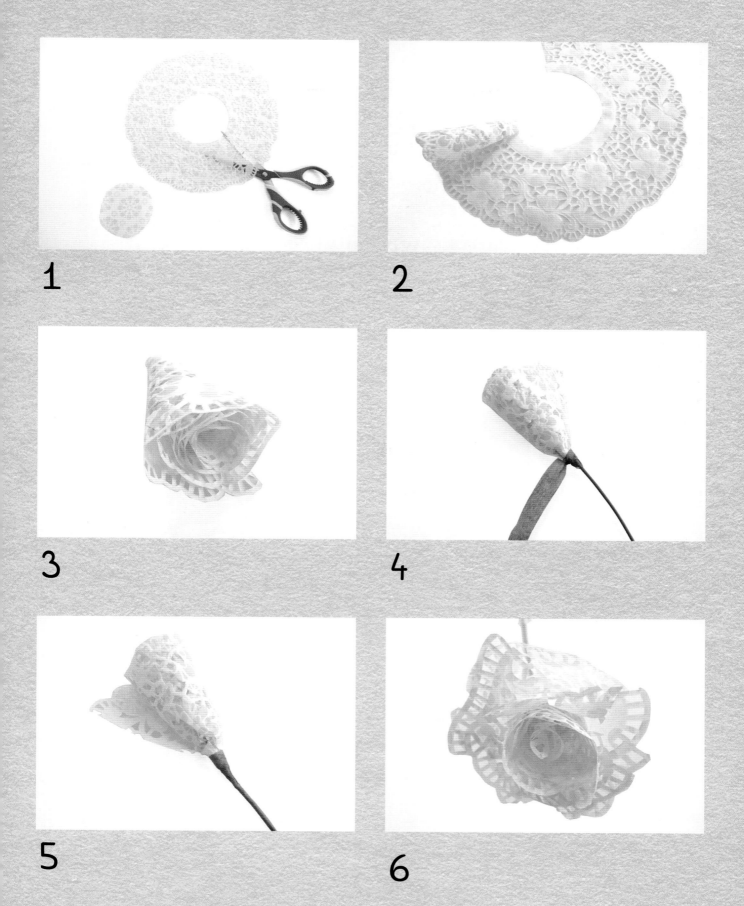

1

2

3

4

5

6

DOILY ROSES

PAPERBACK HEDGEHOG

It takes a little patience folding all the pages in this easy project – but the end result is worth it.

You will need:

- [ ] 1 x old, unwanted paperback book (minimum of 160 pages)
- [ ] 2 x black round beads
- [ ] Small piece of black card
- [ ] Small piece of fawn-coloured card
- [ ] Scissors
- [ ] Clear all-purpose adhesive

1 If your book is quite new, bend the front and back cover right back a few times to break the spine. Open the book at the very first page. Fold this first page in half lengthways so the folded crease is on the left.

2 Take the bottom corner of the first page and fold it so that the centre fold made in Step 1 is perfectly horizontal, creating a triangle shape. The inner edge of your triangle should be in line with the centre of the book.

3 Make the same fold as in Step 2 but at the top of the book to create another triangle shape.

4 Take the next page and continue to fold the pages in exactly the same way as Steps 1 to 3. Keep the folded crease on the left and all your triangles facing the same way.

5 About halfway through the book, start to fold the pages in the opposite direction so you are now folding the pages in half with the lengthways fold on the right. Continue folding and creating triangles until you reach the very end of the book.

6 Using scissors, cut out a semi-circle from the black card, approximately ¾in (2cm) in diameter, for your hedgehog's nose. Then cut out two ¾in (2cm) circles from the fawn-coloured card to make ear shapes. Cut the very bottom of the circle away using scissors and make a small slit to almost halfway up the ear. Add a drop of glue to one side of the slit and stick the other side of the slit on top to make a slight cone shape.

7 Open up your book so all the pages fan out, and glue on the nose and ears. Finally, add a tiny drop of glue to the black beads to stick on the eyes.

Tip Second-hand books are great to use for this project. I found a book about hedgehogs – how perfect is that?

NOW I CAN PAPER CRAFT

1

2

3

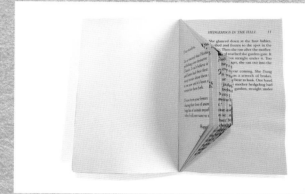

4

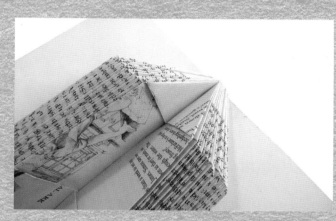

5

6

7

STRAW WREATH

Make this easy festive wreath for Christmas or any other special occasion.

You will need:

- ☐ 1 x A4 piece of thick card
- ☐ 1 x box of 50 straight pink straws (or colour of your choice)
- ☐ 1 x box of 50 straight blue straws (or colour of your choice)
- ☐ Thin ribbon
- ☐ Compass
- ☐ Pencil
- ☐ Craft knife
- ☐ Cutting mat
- ☐ Glue gun and glue sticks

1 Take the piece of thick card and use the pencil and compass to draw an outer circle 7in (18cm) in diameter and an inner circle 3¼in (8cm) in diameter from the same centre point.

2 Using a craft knife on a cutting mat, cut out the outer and inner circles, leaving a ring shape (see How to use a craft knife, page 30).

3 Using pink straws, carefully glue one at the North, South, East and West points on the ring using the glue gun. You will only need to apply a small blob of the hot glue onto the cardboard ring as it is very strong.

4 In the same way, glue four more pink straws centrally between each of the North, South, West and East straws.

5 Stick more pink straws around the ring, working on one section at a time, until you fill the entire ring.

6 Take blue straws and cut approximately 2in (5cm) off each one using the craft knife on a cutting mat.

7 Add a small blob of hot glue approximately ½in (1cm) away from the bottom of the blue straw and stick each shorter blue straw on top of the long pink ones, working your way around the entire ring.

8 Cut a 4in (10cm) piece of thin ribbon and form a small loop. Then using the hot glue gun, stick this loop onto the back of your ring so you are able to hang it up.

9 Finally, decorate your wreath with concertina pinwheels in matching colours. See page 32 for instructions on how to make them.

Tip Warning! Hot glue can burn so make sure you get an adult to help you with this project.

1

2

3

4

5

6

7

8

9

BIRDIE PEG

Use this pretty peg as a bookmark or to keep some favourite photos together.

Find the template on page 116

You will need:

- [ ] 1 x wooden peg
- [ ] 3 x patterned pieces of card with different designs
- [ ] 1 x small button to match your card
- [ ] Cord or thin ribbon
- [ ] Tracing paper
- [ ] Pencil
- [ ] Eraser
- [ ] Scissors
- [ ] Pinking shears
- [ ] Stick glue
- [ ] Clear all-purpose adhesive

1 Trace over the body, breast and wing templates on page 116, using the technique shown on page 26. Cut out the templates and draw round the shapes using the three different patterned cards.

2 Using scissors, cut out each shape. Use the eraser to rub away any pencil lines.

3 Holding the pinking shears at the very end of the bird's tail, cut a zigzag line across it.

4 Use the stick glue to glue the breast and wing onto the body of the bird.

5 Take the button and thread a length of cord or thin ribbon through the buttonhole. Tie a bow at the back of the button.

6 Using clear all-purpose adhesive, apply a tiny dot of glue to the bird's wing. Stick on the button, trapping the bow in place, and leave to dry. Cut the ribbon ends to equal lengths.

7 Add a line of clear all-purpose adhesive to the back of the bird and then press the peg firmly into position. Make sure the button lines up with the top of the peg as this will make it stronger when pressing open the peg.

Tip Paint your wooden peg a bright colour for that extra finishing touch.

94

1

2

3

4

5

6

7

PAPER BEADS

Make beads in different shapes and colours to create funky jewellery.

You will need:

- [ ] 1 x A4 sheet of thin coloured card
- [ ] Ruler
- [ ] Pencil
- [ ] Craft knife
- [ ] Cutting mat
- [ ] Scissors
- [ ] Eraser
- [ ] Cocktail sticks
- [ ] Small paintbrush
- [ ] Stick glue
- [ ] White glue
- [ ] Cord elastic
- [ ] Modelling clay

1 Using a pencil and ruler, measure ¾in (2cm) from the bottom short edge of the card and make a dot. Keep measuring and marking ¾in (2cm) lengths until you reach the other side of the card. Repeat this for the top short edge but also add one ⅜in (1cm) mark right at the start. Starting from the very bottom corner of the card, draw a diagonal line up to the top ⅜in (1cm) mark. Draw a line back down from this point to the first ¾in (2cm) mark to create a triangle. Keep repeating this and draw lots of long triangles across the card.

2 Put the card on a cutting mat. Holding a ruler along the first drawn line, use the craft knife to cut along this line (see How to use a craft knife, page 30). Cut out all the triangles in this way. Use an eraser to rub away any pencil lines that are showing.

3 Take a cocktail stick and place it at the wide base of the triangle. Roll the card around the cocktail stick as tightly as possible.

4 Continue rolling the card around the cocktail stick as evenly and tightly as possible so it starts to form an oval-shaped bead. As you get approximately two thirds of the way up the triangle, add a little stick glue to the remaining exposed card.

5 Finish rolling the card around the cocktail stick to get the final bead shape. The glue will hold the tip of the triangle in place, but as you haven't glued it all the way down, you can manipulate the bead with your fingers into a good symmetrical shape if you need to.

6 Repeat Steps 3 to 5 to make as many beads as you want. Thread a bead onto a cocktail stick and using a small paintbrush, coat white glue all over the bead to seal it. Try not to get glue on the cocktail stick. Push the cocktail stick into modelling clay. Repeat this step for all the beads, making sure the beads do not touch each other once in the modelling clay. Leave to dry.

7 You can make different-shaped beads in the same way, by altering the base length of each triangle. If you measure ⅜in (1cm) lengths along the card in Step 1, you can make smaller, more rounded beads.

8 Cut a piece of cord elastic the length you want for a necklace or bracelet plus an extra 2in (5cm) for tying off. Thread on as many beads as you like. Tie a double knot in the elastic and cut away any excess using scissors. Slide the beads around so the knot is hidden inside the hole of one of the beads.

Tip Mix in beads from broken pieces of jewellery to reuse them and create new designs.

1

2

3

4

5

6

7

8

PAPER BEADS

WOVEN PAPER BASKET

Weave strips of paper to create
a handy home-made basket.

You will need:

- [ ] 1 x A2 sheet of coloured cartridge paper
- [ ] Pencil
- [ ] Ruler
- [ ] Craft knife
- [ ] Cutting mat
- [ ] Masking tape

1 Using a pencil and ruler, mark dots along the long side of the cartridge paper 1in (2.5cm) apart, at both the top and bottom edges. Now join these lines up to create thin strips all 1in by 16.5in (2.5cm x 42cm). Use a craft knife along the ruler's edge on a cutting mat to cut out 12 strips (see How to use a craft knife, page 30).

2 Lay six strips horizontally and six vertically and weave the strips together over and under each other. Using masking tape, mark out a central square shape that will form the bottom of your basket. It will be between the third and fourth strips at each side. Also add little pieces of masking tape to the ends of your strips to hold them together.

3 Place a ruler along one of the masked lines and bend all the strips upwards. Fold right over to make a crease line.

4 Repeat Step 3 on the other sides so you make crease lines forming the bottom of your basket. Carefully remove the masking tape.

5 Hold up all the strips on the left-hand side and on the top side of the square bottom. Three of them on either side will naturally overlap each other. Start to weave these three strips together, working your way up and along to build an entire corner. You will have to keep removing and replacing the small pieces of masking tape holding the strips together at the ends.

Tip Stamp a pattern all over your paper on both sides before cutting it into strips to make a decorative pattern on your weave.

6 Now pick up all of the strips on the right-hand side of the square. Three of those strips will naturally overlap with the remaining three from the top side of the square. Weave these together. Do not worry too much about the evenness of the basket weave, as you can correct that later on.

7 Work your way around the basket, weaving all the corners together. Once you have the final shape you can remove the masking tape pieces and start pulling at the strips to make the sides look the same all the way round.

8 Decide on the height of your basket. Make sure you have enough length on each paper strip to fold back and over the strip that directly crosses it (we shall call this the partner strip) and still have enough length to weave it back through the strips below to secure it in place.

9 Take the partner strip that the first strip is folded behind and woven into from Step 8 and fold this strip behind again. You will be able to weave this strip into the inside of the basket. Again, work your way around the top of the entire basket.

NOW I CAN PAPER CRAFT

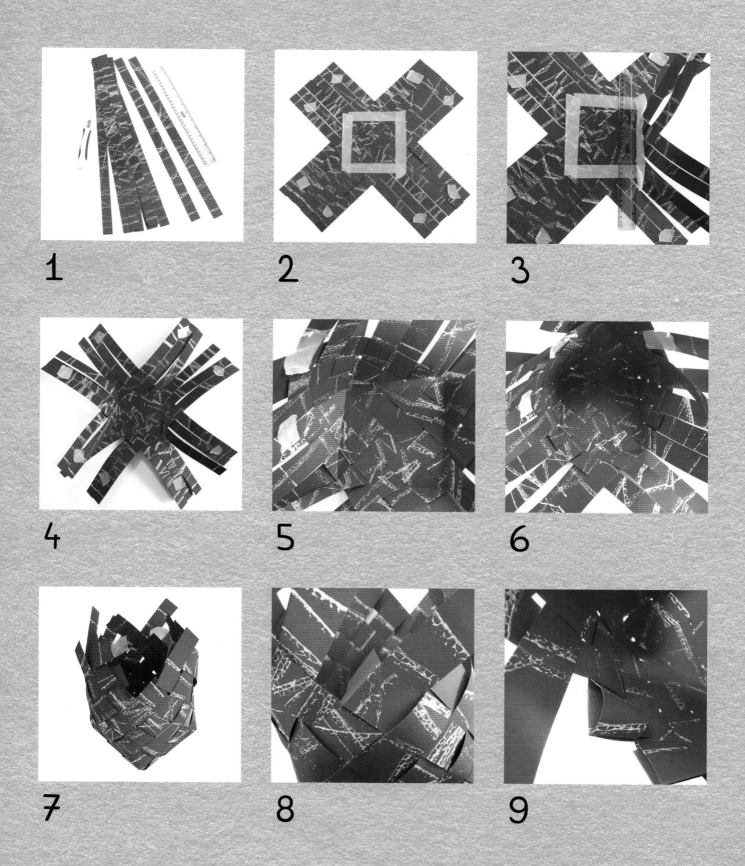

1

2

3

4

5

6

7

8

9

QUILLED FLOWERS

Use a very traditional technique
to make bright hanging flowers.

You will need:

- [ ] 1 x A4 sheet of thin yellow card
- [ ] 1 x A4 sheet of thin orange card
- [ ] 1 x piece of white paper
- [ ] Ruler
- [ ] Craft knife
- [ ] Cutting mat
- [ ] Scissors
- [ ] Stick glue
- [ ] Clear all-purpose adhesive
- [ ] Cocktail sticks
- [ ] Pencil and compass
- [ ] Crochet hook or knitting needle
- [ ] Ribbon

1 Cut six strips approximately ½in (1cm) wide from the long side of your yellow card using a craft knife and ruler on a cutting mat (see How to use a craft knife, page 30).

2 Take one strip and drag it carefully along the edge of one blade of the scissors to make a curl, being careful not to touch the blade with your fingers. Ask an adult to help.

3 Start to wrap the very end of the card strip tightly around a cocktail stick. Continue to wrap the card around itself until you come to the end.

4 Using a pencil and compass, draw a circle of approximately 1in (2.5cm) diameter onto the piece of white paper. Remove the cocktail stick to let the coil of card loosen and unravel itself until it is the same size as this circle. Using the stick glue, glue the very end of the card to secure the spiral. Repeat Steps 2 to 4 for all your yellow strips.

5 Once dry, the centre of each coil will be roughly in the middle of each circle. You need to move the coils so the centre of the coil is at the bottom of your circle. Use the cocktail stick to help you evenly space the coils.

6 Pinch the top section only of the circle, making a crease in three or four of the coils at the top to form a pointed teardrop shape. Repeat Steps 5 and 6 to shape all of your yellow coiled circles.

7 To make the central coil, cut one ½in (1cm) wide strip from the long edge of your orange card. Curl it along the blade of your scissors as in Step 2, then spiral the whole length around a cocktail stick as in Step 3. Let the coil loosen slightly and glue the end to form a small coiled circle. Place all your petal shapes around it so the points face outwards.

8 To make a hanging loop, cut one more ½in (1cm) wide strip of yellow card, but this time from the remaining width of the card. Start to spiral the very end around a knitting needle or crochet hook. Glue the end in place with stick glue. Now, using clear all-purpose adhesive, stick all the petals to the central coil and the hanging loop to one of the petals. Leave to dry on a flat surface. Finally, tie a length of ribbon through the loop so you can hang your flower up.

Tip Follow Steps 1 to 5 and then pinch the rolled card in different places to make other petal shapes.

NOW I CAN PAPER CRAFT

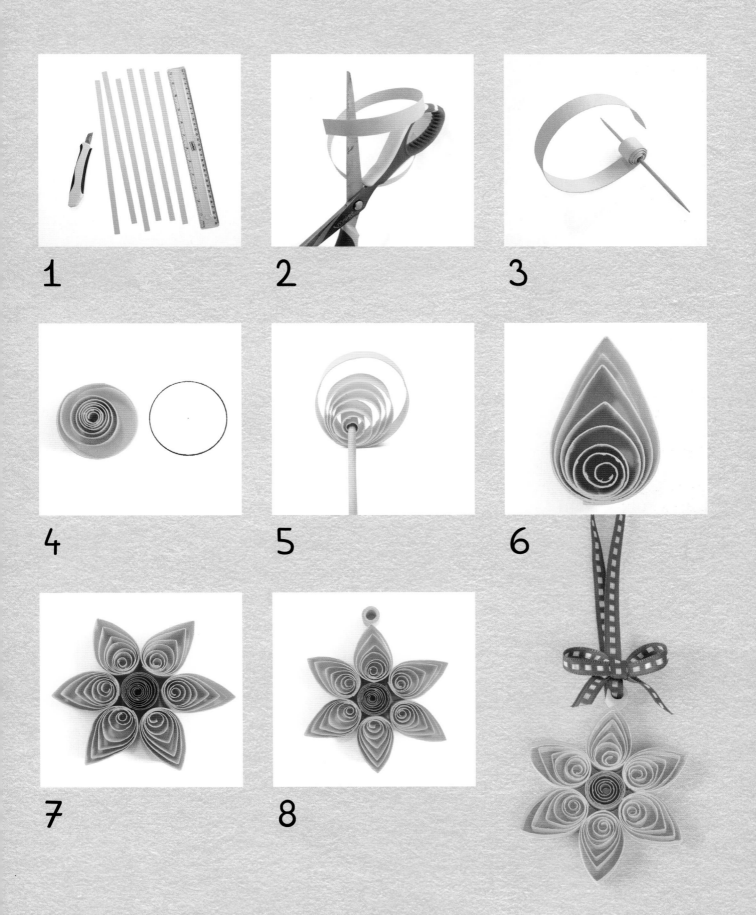

1

2

3

4

5

6

7

8

STAG'S HEAD

Master the art of folding and make a great trophy for your wall!

Find the templates on pages 121–3

You will need:

- [ ] 1 x A3 piece of thin card
- [ ] 1 x A4 piece of corrugated cardboard
- [ ] Patterned paper (optional)
- [ ] Tracing paper
- [ ] Double-sided tape
- [ ] String
- [ ] Ruler
- [ ] Craft knife
- [ ] Cutting mat
- [ ] Scissor
- [ ] Stick glue
- [ ] Clear all-purpose adhesive

Tip You can cover the stag's head in patterned paper instead of painting it, but you'd need to glue the paper to the card before you start cutting and folding.

1 Photocopy the stag's head template on page 123. Using stick glue, glue this paper copy onto an A3 piece of thin card and roughly cut out the shape using scissors to make it easier to handle. Alternatively, photocopy the template directly onto thin card, then cut it out. Keep the excess pieces of card as you will need them in Step 8.

2 Cut pieces of double-sided tape and stick onto all the tabs illustrated on the template. You do not need to make the tape the exact size and shape of each tab.

3 Using a craft knife along a ruler's edge on a cutting mat, carefully cut around all the edges of the template (see How to use a craft knife, page 30).

4 Using the back of the blade of the scissors against the ruler, carefully score a fold line along all the fold lines marked on the template (see How to score for folding, page 29).

5 Fold all the creases so you can check you haven't missed any and to make the shape very easy to manipulate.

6 Peel the backing off all of the pieces of double-sided tape on all of your tabs.

7 Starting on one side of the stag's head, stick the tabs to the corresponding shapes. Work your way around to the nose and back up to the other side of the head before you finally stick on the back of the head. This enables you to get your fingers into the shape and firmly press the tape to hold it in position.

8 Photocopy or trace over the antlers and ears templates on page 122 using the technique shown on page 26 and transfer them onto the excess card left in Step 1. Cut them out using scissors. As you did in Step 4, score along the marked lines and fold into shape.

9 Photocopy or trace over the shield template on page 121 and cut it out. Draw round the shape onto the A4 piece of corrugated card and cut it out. Using clear all-purpose adhesive, glue a piece of string to the back of the cardboard shield at the top so you can hang it up. Again using the clear all-purpose adhesive, stick the ears and antlers onto the head, and glue the finished head onto the shield. Your stag's head is now ready to paint.

Tip This template can be adapted to make a zebra, horse or even a unicorn's head!

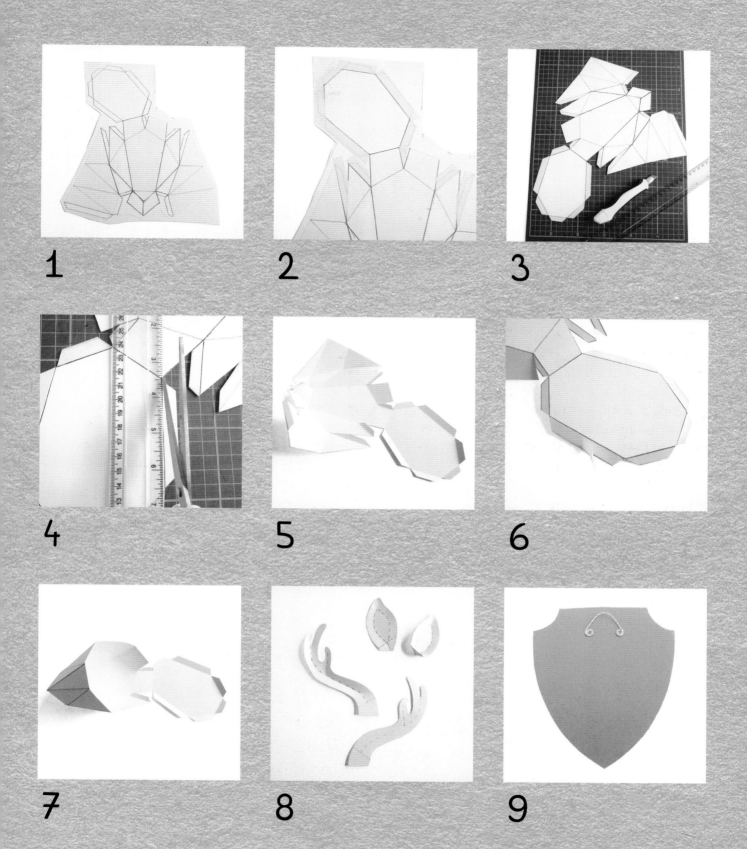

1

2

3

4

5

6

7

8

9

ORIGAMI LIGHTS

Have a go at origami to make these gorgeous flower fairy-light covers.

You will need:

- [ ] 10 x A4 sheets of patterned tracing paper
- [ ] Battery-operated LED fairy lights (10 bulbs)
- [ ] Ruler
- [ ] Pencil
- [ ] Craft knife
- [ ] Cutting mat
- [ ] Double-sided tape

Tip Remember to always turn fairy lights off if you are leaving the room.

1 Using a ruler and pencil, draw six squares 4 x 4in (10 x 10cm) in size onto the sheets of patterned tracing paper. Cut out all the squares using the craft knife along the ruler's edge on a cutting mat (see How to use a craft knife, page 30). Take one square and fold it in half on the diagonal, corner to opposite corner, to form a triangle shape.

2 Fold the left- and right-hand points of the triangle inwards to meet the top point, forming a square shape. Press the folds with your fingers.

3 Fold the same two points back down on themselves so their edges meet along the bottom edge of the square shape.

4 Open out the folded corners created in Steps 2 and 3. Press them flat with your fingers so you are reversing the fold along the existing creases to create kite shapes either side.

5 Fold the top corners of the kite shapes down on each side so the top edges are level with the edges of the square shape behind.

6 Fold both sides of the former kite shape from the outside edge in, to meet the inside edge of the fold. Place a piece of double-sided tape along one of the folded edges.

7 Peel the backing off the double-sided tape. Now gently curve the sides of the entire square shape until the sides meet each other and they stick together.

8 Repeat Steps 1 to 7 (apart from the cutting out) to make five more folded petal shapes. Cut strips of double-sided tape and stick them along one edge of each petal shape. Remove the backing and start to stick them together so they form the overall flower shape.

9 As you work your way around the flower, a hole will naturally start to appear in the centre. Before adding your last petal, take a fairy-light bulb and squeeze it into this central hole so that ¼in (5mm) of the LED bulb pokes out of the top of the flower, with the cable hanging out from the bottom. Add the last remaining petal, trapping the bulb in place. Repeat Steps 1 to 9 to make nine more flowers to add to your fairy-light string and cover all the bulbs.

NOW I CAN PAPER CRAFT

1

2

3

4

5

6

7

8

9

TEMPLATES

Here are all the templates you need for the projects. Photocopy them at 100%, unless otherwise stated, then cut them out.

Birdie peg (see page 92)

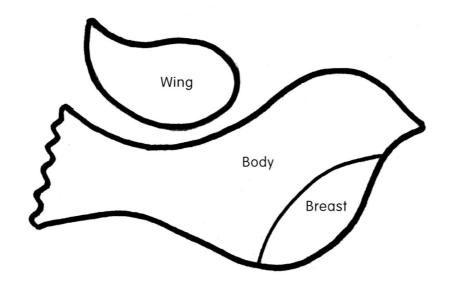

NOW I CAN PAPER CRAFT

Pretty wallet (see page 68)
Photocopy at 115%

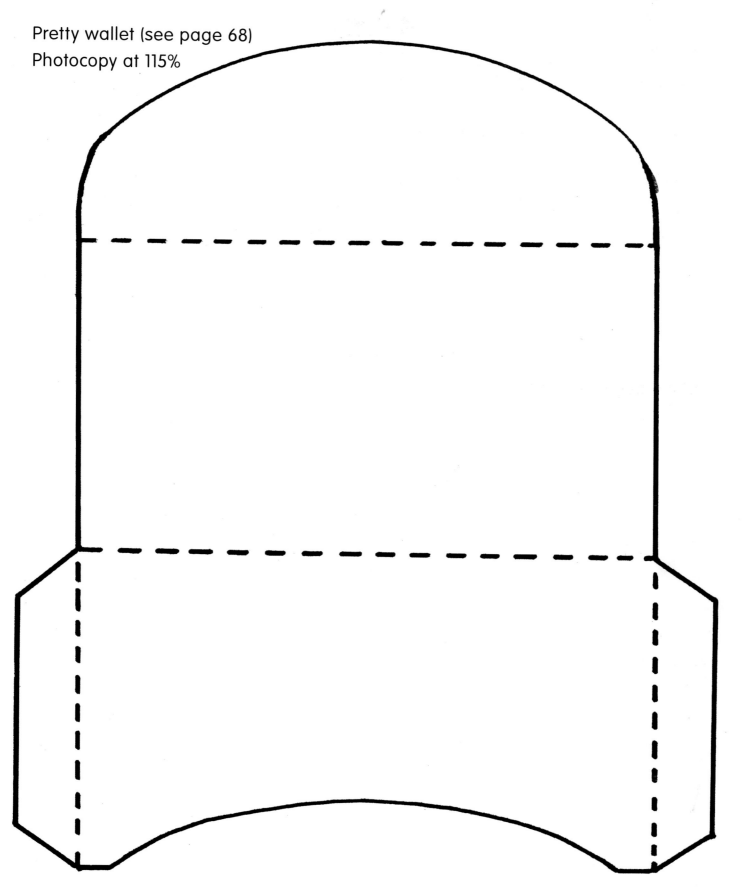

Map mobile (see page 56)

NOW I CAN PAPER CRAFT

Owl lantern (see page 72)
Photocopy at 115%

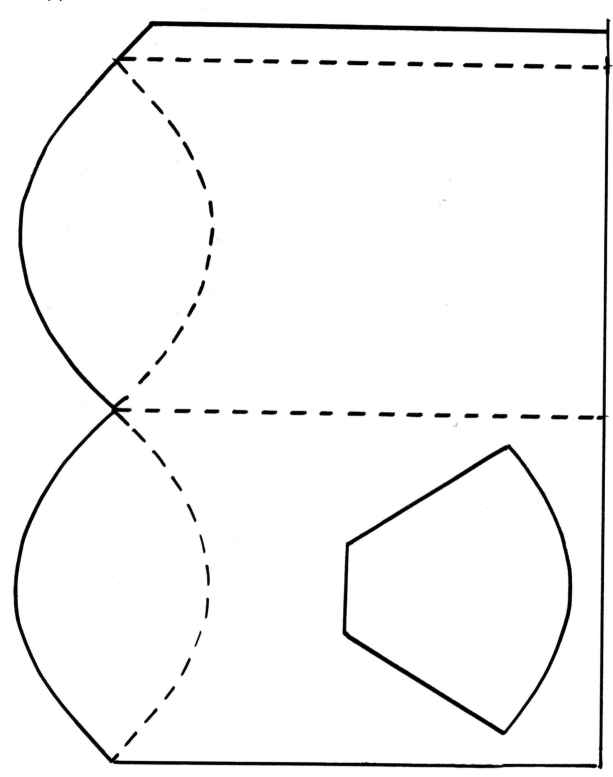

Dancing teddy bear (see page 48)

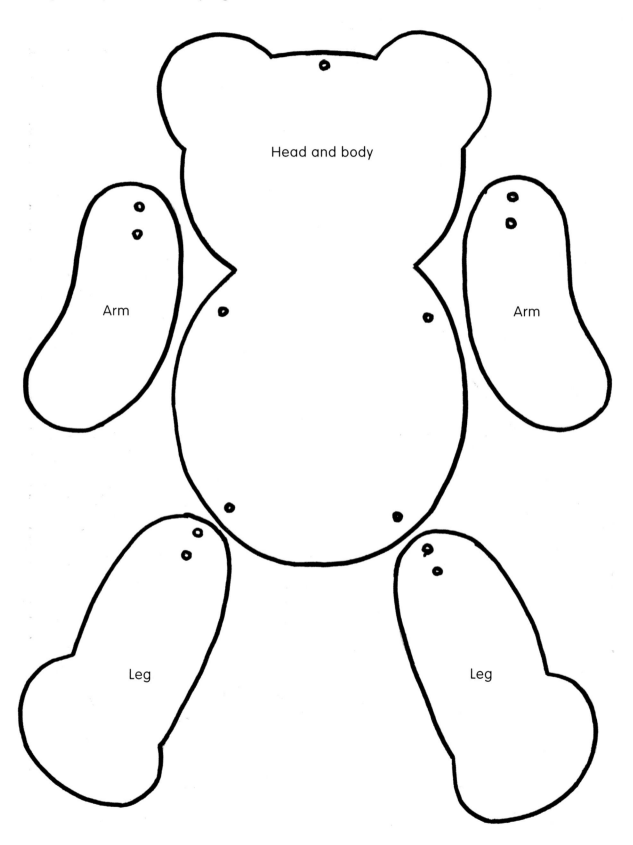

Head and body

Arm

Arm

Leg

Leg

NOW I CAN PAPER CRAFT

Stag's head (see page 108)
Photocopy at 141%

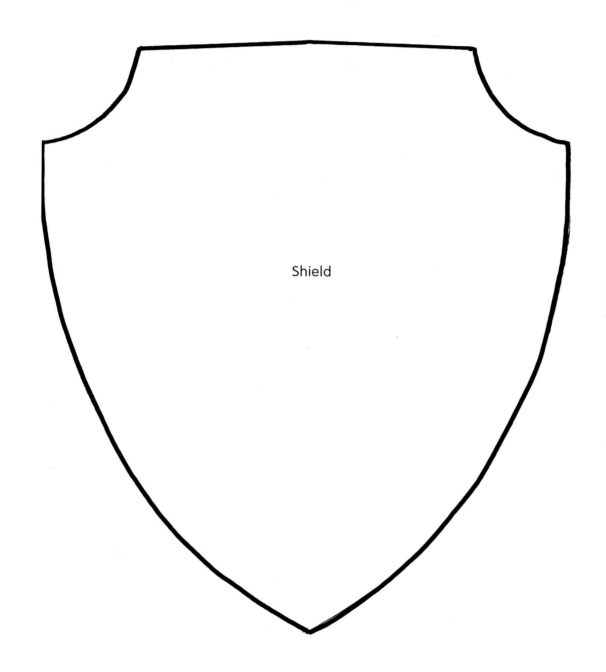

Shield

Stag's head (see page 108)
Photocopy at 141%

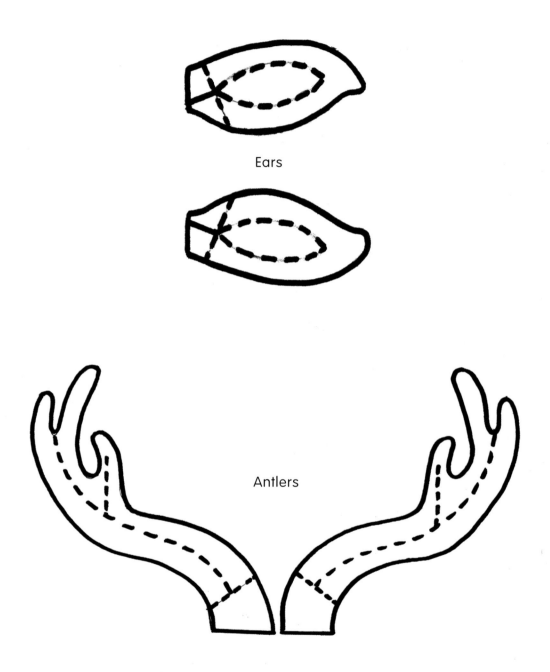

Ears

Antlers

NOW I CAN PAPER CRAFT

Stag's head (see page 108)
Photocopy at 141%

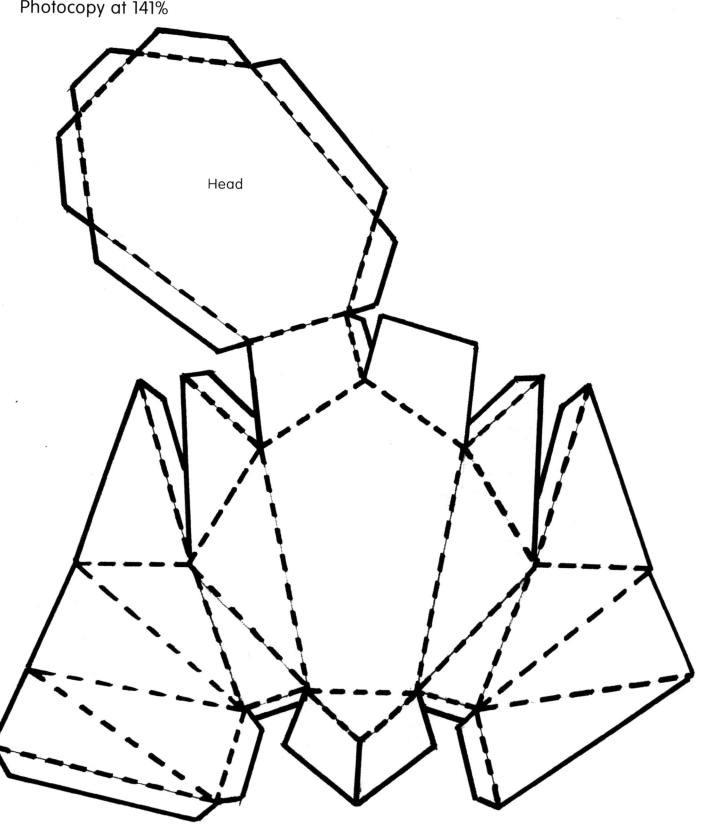

Head

RESOURCES

UK

Craft Superstore
(Online store)
www.craftsuperstore.co.uk

Hobbycraft
(Stores nationwide)
www.hobbycraft.co.uk

Minerva Crafts
(Online store)
www.minervacrafts.com

The Range
(Stores nationwide)
www.therange.co.uk

Wilko
(Stores nationwide)
www.wilko.com

USA

Hobby Lobby
(Stores nationwide)
www.hobbylobby.com

Jo-Ann fabric and craft
(Stores nationwide)
www.joann.com

Michaels
(Stores nationwide)
www.michaels.com

Walmart
(Stores nationwide)
www.walmart.com

ABOUT THE AUTHOR

Tansy Wilson has a BA (Hons) in 3D Design. After graduating, she set up her own business making jewellery and home decorations. She is also a qualified teacher and works at the University of the Arts in London as an external moderator for art and design subjects. Tansy loves making things out of paper and spends a lot of her free time trying out different techniques. She writes articles and creates projects for the magazine *Making Jewellery* and has written three jewellery books for beginners, also available from GMC Publications.

INDEX

A
accordion pleats 28

B
balloons 25
beads 24
Birdie peg 92–95, 116
bows 22
buttons 24

C
card 18, 19
cocktail sticks 16
compass 11
craft knife 10, 30
crochet hook 17
curtain ring 21
cutting mat 10

D
Dancing teddy bear
  48–51, 120
découpage paper 19
doilies 22
Doily roses 80–83

E
elastic 24
embroidery ring 24
equipment 10–17, 20
erasers 17
eyes 21

F
fairy lights 20
floristry wire 16
folding 29

G
glue 14
glue gun 15
googly eyes 21

H
hand stamps 11
hole punch 12
hole reinforcers 19

L
lights 20

M
Map mobile 56–59, 118
maps 21
materials 18–25
modelling clay 16

O
Origami lights 112–115
Owl lantern 72–75, 119

P
paintbrushes 12
paints 13
paper 18, 19
paperbacks 21
Paperback hedgehog 84–87
Paper beads 96–99
paper fasteners 17, 31
Paper-plate masks 44–47
paper plates 22
paper straws 23
Paper windmill 40–43
pegs 25
pencils 12
pens 12
photo frames 20
Piggy bank 60–63
pinking shears 11
pins 17
pinwheels 32–33
pipe cleaners 23
Pleated moths 64–67
pleats 28
Pop-up monster cards 36–39

Pretty wallet 68–71, 117
punches 11

Q
Quilled flowers 104–107

R
recycled paper and card 19, 21
resources 124
ribbons 22
Rolled-paper bowl 76–79
ruler 10

S
scissors 11
scoring for folding 29
Stag's head 108–111, 121–123
stamps 11
Straw wreath 88–91
straws 23
string 23

T
tape 15
tea lights 20
techniques 26–33
templates 26–27, 116–123
3D butterfly picture 52–55
tools 10–17
tracing a template 26–27
tracing paper 18
transferring a template 26–27

U
using a craft knife 30
using paper fasteners 31

V
varnish 13

W
Woven paper basket 100–103